winter
cooking

BRIDGET JONES

using the season's finest ingredients

winter cooking

LORENZ BOOKS

NOTES
Bracketed terms are intended for American readers.

For all recipes, quantities are given in both metric and imperial measures and, where appropriate, measures are also given in standard cups and spoons. Follow one set, but not a mixture, because they are not interchangeable.

Standard spoon and cup measures are level. 1 tsp = 5ml, 1 tbsp = 15ml, 1 cup = 250ml|8fl oz

Australian standard tablespoons are 20ml. Australian readers should use 3 tsp in place of 1 tbsp for measuring small quantities of gelatine, flour, salt, etc.

Medium (US large) eggs are used unless otherwise stated.

This edition is published by Lorenz Books

Lorenz Books is an imprint of Anness Publishing Ltd
Hermes House, 88–89 Blackfriars Road, London SE1 8HA
tel. 020 7401 2077; fax 020 7633 9499; www.lorenzbooks.com; info@anness.com

© Anness Publishing Ltd 2003

UK agent: The Manning Partnership Ltd, 6 The Old Dairy, Melcombe Road, Bath BA2 3LR; tel. 01225 478444; fax 01225 478440; sales@manning-partnership.co.uk

UK distributor: Grantham Book Services Ltd, Isaac Newton Way, Alma Park Industrial Estate, Grantham, Lincs NG31 9SD; tel. 01476 541080; fax 01476 541061; orders@gbs.tbs-ltd.co.uk

North American agent/distributor: National Book Network, 4501 Forbes Boulevard, Suite 200, Lanham, MD 20706; tel. 301 459 3366; fax 301 429 5746; www.nbnbooks.com

Australian agent/distributor: Pan Macmillan Australia, Level 18, St Martins Tower, 31 Market St, Sydney, NSW 2000; tel. 1300 135 113; fax 1300 135 103; customer.service@macmillan.com.au

New Zealand agent/distributor: David Bateman Ltd, 30 Tarndale Grove, Off Bush Road, Albany, Auckland; tel. (09) 415 7664; fax (09) 415 8892

A CIP catalogue record for this book is available from the British Library.

PUBLISHER: Joanna Lorenz
MANAGING EDITOR: Judith Simons
PROJECT EDITOR: Katy Bevan
COPY EDITOR: Sarah Brown
DESIGNER: Adelle Morris
PRODUCTION CONTROLLER: Darren Price
PHOTOGRAPHERS: Martin Brigdale, James Duncan, Gus Filgate, Michelle Garrett, Don Last, William Lingwood, Patrick McLeavey, Thomas Odulate, Craig Robertson, Jo Whitworth
RECIPES: Maxine Clark, Joanna Farrow, Christine Ingram, Lucy Knox, Keith Richond, Rena Salaman, Simon Smith, Ysanne Spevack, Linda Tubby, Steven Wheeler

10 9 8 7 6 5 4 3 2 1

CONTENTS

INTRODUCTION

Winter is the season for inner warmth, when sharing good things brings a positive glow of goodwill to dull days. Traditions focus on entertaining at home, sharing simple, warming suppers and gathering for Saturday dinner or Sunday lunch. Everyday meals are generally more substantial than at other times of the year.

This is the season to indulge in comforting nursery foods, but these days there is also an urge to balance them with lighter dishes with a modern twist. While the weather is cold and crisp, hot and healthy meals fuel invigorating walks and energetic snow sports. When spirits flag, steaming hot broth, healing drinks and tempting toddies are soothing restoratives.

Winter goodness

While global distribution systems mean that virtually all ingredients are obtainable throughout the year, concentrating on food from close to home is the way to eat affordable, good-quality meals with maximum food value. Focusing on seasonal produce is sensible for a healthy diet because the type of foods that nature makes available complement the body's needs. As the weather becomes cold, energy-giving foods and ingredients for hot dishes are more plentiful.

FISH AND SEAFOOD
Supplies of some fresh fish and seafood can be unreliable when fleets cannot venture into rough seas. Oysters and mussels are good winter shellfish. Smoked fish, such as trout, mackerel and kippers are versatile, and preserved herrings (pickled in vinegar or salted and packed in oil) are a good store-cupboard standby for supper dishes or appetizers. Fresh fish such as red mullet and turbot are also available in the winter months.

MEAT, POULTRY AND GAME

Goose is the seasonal poultry to enjoy during winter months; its dark flesh complemented by rich wine gravies and tangy fruit sauces. Fresh whole turkey is a favourite choice for celebrations. Guinea fowl (now farmed) is a tasty alternative to chicken for roasting, and mature pheasants make excellent casseroles.

Seasons for wild deer overlap, and farmed venison is always available, but winter is when this rich, dark meat is really popular. Large roasts taken from the haunch are very grand; succulent casseroles, and steaks braised in rich sauces are particularly good for winter dinner parties. Baked ham or gammon on the bone is commonly served as the centrepiece of a cold buffet but is also good hot. Beef and pork are also popular for casseroles and stews.

Full-flavoured casseroles, meat sauces, sausages and pâtés using liver, kidneys and other types of offal are welcome for everyday meals. Scottish haggis, (a spicy sausage made with offal and oats), is good with a rich whisky sauce. Grilled or pan-fried kidneys are a special choice for leisurely weekend breakfasts, especially with bacon, eggs, hash browns or rösti, succulent sausages and mushrooms.

VERSATILE VEGETABLES

Roots and tubers are satisfying and versatile ingredients in winter cooking. Large fluffy potatoes bake well and make excellent hot-pot toppings and roast wedges. Jerusalem artichokes, parsnips and swedes are on top form. Pass on frilly greens and opt for flavoursome winter cabbage, kale and Brussels sprouts. Sprouted beans and seeds are delicious in stir-fries or salads and are an excellent source of vitamin C. Chestnuts can be roasted as a snack or boiled, peeled and used as a vegetable. They are delicious hot with winter greens and zesty orange or combined with dried fruit in stuffings or pilaff.

WINTER FRUIT

The citrus season in January and February brings Seville or Bigarade oranges that are used for that essentially British preserve, marmalade. These bitter fruits also make full-flavoured savoury sauces and relishes, such as Bigarade sauce to go with roast duck. Tangerines, including mandarins, clementines and satsumas, are juicy and full of flavour, as are seedless navel or navelina oranges. Catch fresh cranberries while they are available, and make the most of pomegranates and pineapples, which are good in early winter. Bananas, apples and kiwi fruit are good everyday snacks or dessert ingredients, with exotic fruit providing extra variety when it is available.

Dried fruit and nuts are harvested and dried in the late autumn and winter months. Good in both savoury and dessert recipes, they are often associated with seasonal celebrations. Apricots, peaches, prunes, dates and figs make warming compotes, pies and bakes.

Hot tips for a Winter chill

Covered markets are vibrant areas in towns and cities and ideal for relaxed winter shopping. They provide a colourful backdrop for butchers, bakers and the smallest of local producers. Shop early in the day, because local cheeses, the best offers from butchers and the most popular home-baked breads, pies and cakes sell quickly.

Small to medium producers of seasonal specialities and high-quality ingredients, such as poultry, meat, game, cheese, confectionery and premium preserves, offer mail-order services, or home delivery through internet ordering. This is particularly useful for foods that have to be ordered in advance anyway, such as fresh goose or turkey, or large cuts of meat.

FUSS-FREE SIMMERING

It is a myth that many long-cooked classic dishes are demanding. With a little forethought, the ingredients can be put to simmer and left virtually unattended for anything from 1–4 hours. Softening or browning onions, vegetables and meat first is necessary for sauces and moist dishes that are cooked for about an hour. For incredible depth of flavour, invest in a big ovenproof cooking pot with a close-fitting lid. Simply mix or layer all the ingredients in the pot with herbs and seasoning. Bring the liquid (water, stock or wine) to the boil before pouring it into the pot. Cover closely and cook until the liquid is just about to boil, then continue to cook gently in the oven or on top of the stove for 2–4 hours, depending on the ingredients. Casseroles with meat or pulses can be cooked for up to 5 hours for rich and succulent results.

- Raw spices, such as whole, crushed or ground coriander and whole or ground cumin, should be cooked briefly in a little oil or butter before they are simmered, as they can taste slightly harsh, particularly when used in significant quantities.

- Herbs and spices with warm flavours are ideal for winter stews and sauces. Rosemary, bay and marjoram; juniper, cinnamon, nutmeg and mace are excellent winter aromatics. Juniper is a favourite for venison, and beef or pork stews with a gamey flavour.

- Bake little rounds of bread spread with butter and mustard until crisp and golden, then serve as a topping for juicy dishes to add contrasting texture.

- Add canned beans and pulses to long-cooked hot pots to turn them into satisfying one-pot meals. Borlotti, cannellini, flageolet and kidney beans or chickpeas are delicious with rich sauces.

- Stir-fried greens are a quick and easy accompaniment to long-cooked casseroles. Shred kale or cabbage and stir-fry briefly with a sprinkling of caraway or fennel seeds.

Restorative recipes

On a cold day, there's nothing like a pot of broth to fill the senses and satisfy the appetite. Just one steaming bowlful brings an inimitable sense of wellbeing. Chicken and beef make fabulous broth; the secret lies in selecting cuts on the bone, roasting very briefly at a high temperature until brown for a rich flavour, then simmering gently with large chunks of onion, carrot, celery, a long twist of lemon rind and several bay leaves. Once strained, the meat should be diced, and lots of diced or shredded vegetables added to the broth and cooked gently. Served with chunks of soda bread, toasted muffins or well-risen cheese scones, a good broth makes a great meal.

Warming toddies are the best body-warmers. The old favourite, whisky toddy, consists of a tot of whisky, several slices of lemon, a good squeeze of lemon juice and a couple of spoons of honey topped up with boiling water. Renowned for soothing a sore throat and clearing the head, the warm whisky has a soporific effect. For a modern, alcohol-free alternative, flavour a toddy with a few sprigs of fresh or dried rosemary and slices of orange and honey. Thin slices of fresh root ginger, lemon and honey make a punchy toddy, while hot apple juice, orange slices, cinnamon and honey make a warming cup that can be spiked with a little brandy for an extra kick.

Wonderful winter salads

An eclectic approach introduces the winter salad as a celebration of flavour, form and texture. Judicious use of pulses, whether soaked and cooked for the appropriate time, or pre-cooked in a can, gives a salad the protein boost it needs to make it more satisfying for winter appetites. Spices, seeds and preserved produce transform diced roots and tubers; nutty oils and rich vinegar dress without masking the flavour of the salad; and hot toppings transform salads into seriously good main courses.

PARING, DICING OR SHREDDING

Cutting techniques make all the difference to the finished dish. Potatoes, carrots and swedes can be cooked until tender, and diced when warm or cool for winter salads; opt for large or small dice depending on the texture required.

- Peel, finely dice and pan-fry potatoes, or par-boiled Jerusalem artichokes in a little sunflower oil, stirring frequently, until browned and tender but firm. Season and toss with cold ingredients just before serving.

- Use a vegetable peeler to pare carrots into ribbons, then soak these in iced water until they curl. Toss them with a sweet-sour dressing flavoured with orange, and roasted fennel seeds just before serving.

- Finely slice or dice canned water chestnuts, or cut them into thin strips, and add them to tender cooked vegetables or winter greens for a super-crunchy texture.

ALTERNATIVE GREENS

When the light salad leaves of summer are out of season, it is time to turn to the greens that are in favour. Cabbages come in many varieties, and the paler ones are more suited to making variations on coleslaw.

- Finely shred wedges of firm winter cabbage, using the heart rather than the outer leaves; white and red cabbage are delicious shredded finely or coarsely.

- Use bean sprouts for bulk, texture and a light flavour with the more expensive leaves such as rocket (arugula), mizuna or watercress.

FRUIT FLAVOURS

Citrus scents are a boon to the winter salad maker, and exotic fruits are available from hotter climates. Use them in dressings to replace the vinegar, or sliced in the dish itself, to add an extra zing, and to compliment the flavour of cold meats.

- Pomegranate seeds are delicious in all sorts of salads. Try them with pan-fried poultry, bacon, pancetta or pork strips; tangy goat's cheese or lively blue cheese; crunchy red cabbage and finely cut raw onion; or chickpeas, barley or wheat.

- Finely slice and then dice thin-skinned winter lemons and limes to bring brilliant bursts of flavour to all sorts of salads. Remove pips (seeds) when slicing the fruit. This is especially good with smoked fish, chickpeas or pan-fried diced gammon.

- Chopped dried apricots and dates are excellent with cheese, poultry or salami and other preserved meats. Other kinds of preserved fruits available include mangoes, apple slices, banana chips and papayas.

HOT DRESSING TIPS

Try tossing a full-flavoured hot dressing into cold ingredients when serving a salad.

- Fry diced bacon until crisp in a little sunflower oil. Remove from the pan with a slotted spoon and cook chopped garlic, a little chopped onion and shredded orange rind in the fat remaining in the pan for a few seconds. Whisk in some balsamic vinegar, freshly ground black pepper, a good pinch of sugar and a little mustard. Whisk in a little olive oil and bring to the boil. Remove from the heat, then drizzle over finely shredded Brussels sprouts or green cabbage and bean sprouts. Sprinkle with the bacon.

- Make a hot chilli dressing by cooking a finely chopped seeded fresh green chilli in a little olive oil with chopped garlic and grated lime rind. Whisk in lime juice, olive oil, seasoning and a little sugar or honey. Remove from the heat when hot. Good with poultry, fish, cheese or root vegetables.

TEMPTING TOPPINGS

The ubiquitous croutons are good on salads, but there are alternatives that turn the simplest vegetable combinations into substantial snacks or meals.

- Cut Welsh rarebit (cheese on toast) into neat squares and serve on a salad of white cabbage, carrot and watercress.

- Grill goat's cheese on slices of French baton or on English muffins. Cut the muffins into little wedges and serve with a salad of coarsely grated carrot and mixed sprouted seeds.

- Grill mashed canned sardines with garlic on thin toast and cut into fingers as a topping for potato salad. Cut the potatoes into fingers, rather than dice, and toss with an olive oil and lemon dressing, adding plenty of grated lemon rind to the dressing.

- Serve small bite-sized meatballs as a salad topping – good with greens or roots.

The thing about puddings

Call them old-fashioned but, in truth, hot puddings have never gone out of favour. We swoon at the first burst of aromatic steam from one of those peculiarly British savoury puddings, filled with steak and kidney, chicken scented with sage and lemon, or bacon and onion. We crave sweet puddings – light golden sponge trickling with treacle or mysteriously dark with chocolate; or fluffy suet pastry speckled with succulent dried fruits or swirled with fruity jam, topped with steaming vanilla custard.

PUDDING PERFECTION

Sponge puddings are amazingly simple to make. The ingredients can be beaten in stages, or at one go, using an electric beater, then spooned into a large cooking basin, covered with foil and steamed for 1–1½hours.

Suet (chilled, grated shortening) pastry requires no rubbing, layering or folding, just mixing and rolling out. It can be filled and rolled up Swiss-roll style, or used to line a basin and filled. Everyone thinks of steaming as the main method of cooking for suet puddings, but they cook wonderfully well in the oven, becoming spongy and forming a light but crisp golden crust when baked. Fillings for baked puddings should be pre-cooked or quick to cook, as the baking time is far shorter than steaming (about 45 minutes). The pastry can be covered the whole time it is in the oven, but uncovering it for the final 15 minutes or so allows it to brown.

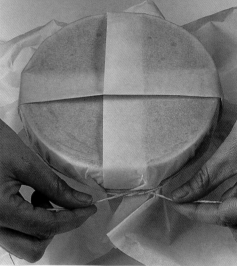

SO-SIMPLE SUET PASTRY

• Always use self-raising (self-rising) flour, or baking powder with plain (all-purpose) flour. Unlike other pastries, suet pastry relies on the raising agent for its light texture.

• Stir the suet into the flour, then mix in just enough water or milk to make a soft but not sticky dough.

• Roll the dough out lightly on a well-floured surface – the cooler it stays and the less it is handled, the lighter it will be.

• When lining a basin or bowl, save about a third for the lid, then roll out the rest of the pastry about 10cm|4in larger than the top of the basin. Dust the pastry lightly with flour and fold into quarters, then place this wedge of pastry in the basin, with the point in the middle of the base. Open out the pastry to line the basin, leaving the excess pastry overhanging the edge. When the pudding is filled, roll out the reserved pastry into a round large enough to cover the filling, and place it on top, pressing it lightly to the rim. Brush the edge with water and fold the overhanging pastry over the edge to seal in the filling.

• For a roly-poly, roll out the pastry to about 5mm|¼in thick and spread with filling, leaving a border of about 2.5cm|1in around the edge. Fold the edge over the filling and brush with a little water before rolling up the pastry and filling.

• Wrap a roly-poly in greased baking parchment and foil for cooking, keeping it loose to allow the pastry to rise, but folding the foil firmly together to keep the moisture in.

tempting
and appetizing

As the days get shorter and colder, appetites sharpen.
Enjoy first courses and side dishes that make the most
of the new season's root vegetables and lift salads with
the energizing flavours of citrus and ground spices.

Root vegetables form the base of this chunky and filling minestrone-style soup. Vary the vegetables according to what you have to hand.

WINTER FARMHOUSE SOUP

INGREDIENTS
serves four

30ml | 2 tbsp olive oil

1 onion, roughly chopped

3 carrots, cut into large chunks

175–200g | 6–7oz turnips, cut into chunks

175g | 6oz swede (rutabaga) cut into chunks

400g | 14oz can chopped Italian tomatoes

15ml | 1 tbsp tomato purée (paste)

5ml | 1 tsp dried mixed herbs

5ml | 1 tsp dried oregano

50g | 2oz dried (bell) peppers, washed and thinly sliced (optional)

1.5 litres | 2½ pints | 6¼ cups vegetable stock or water

50g | 2oz | ½ cup dried macaroni

400g | 14 oz can red kidney beans, rinsed and drained

30ml | 2 tbsp chopped fresh flat leaf parsley

sea salt and ground black pepper

freshly grated Parmesan cheese to serve

1 Heat the olive oil in a large pan, add the onion and cook over a low heat for about 5 minutes, until softened. Add the carrot, turnip, swede chunks, canned chopped tomatoes, tomato purée, dried mixed herbs, dried oregano and dried peppers, if using. Stir in a little salt and plenty of pepper to taste.

2 Pour in the vegetable stock or water and bring to the boil. Stir well, cover the pan, then lower the heat and simmer for 30 minutes, stirring occasionally.

3 Add the pasta to the pan and bring quickly to the boil, stirring. Lower the heat and simmer, uncovered, for about 8 minutes, until the pasta is only just tender, or according to the instructions on the packet. Stir frequently.

4 Stir in the kidney beans. Heat through for 2–3 minutes, then remove the pan from the heat and stir in the parsley. Taste the soup for seasoning. Serve hot in warmed soup bowls, with grated cheese handed around separately.

Vegetables roasted in olive oil give this winter soup a wonderful depth of flavour. You can use other vegetables if you wish, or adapt the quantities, depending on what you have to hand.

ROASTED ROOT VEGETABLE SOUP

1 Preheat the oven to 200°C | 400°F | Gas 6. Put the olive oil into a large bowl. Add the prepared vegetables and toss until coated in the oil.

2 Spread out the vegetables in a single layer on one large or two small baking sheets. Tuck the bay leaves and the thyme and rosemary sprigs among the vegetables.

3 Roast the vegetables for about 50 minutes, until tender, turning them occasionally to make sure they brown evenly. Remove from the oven, discard the herbs and transfer the vegetables to a large pan.

4 Pour the stock into the pan and bring to the boil. Reduce the heat, season to taste, then simmer for 10 minutes. Transfer the soup to a food processor or blender (or use a hand blender) and process for a few minutes, until thick and smooth.

5 Return the soup to the pan to heat through. Season and serve with a swirl of sour cream. Garnish each serving with a sprig of thyme.

COOK'S TIP Dried herbs can be used in place of fresh; sprinkle 2.5ml | ½ tsp of each over the vegetables in step 2.

INGREDIENTS
serves six

50ml | 2fl oz | ¼ cups olive oil

1 small butternut squash, peeled, seeded and cubed

2 carrots, cut into thick rounds

1 large parsnip, cubed

1 small swede (rutabaga), cubed

2 leeks, thickly sliced

1 onion, quartered

3 bay leaves

4 thyme sprigs, plus extra to garnish

3 rosemary sprigs

1.2 litres | 2 pints | 5 cups vegetable stock

salt and ground black pepper

sour cream, to serve

These versatile and delicious filo pastry parcels are an excellent way of using up small pieces of cooked turkey – a useful idea if you have lots of turkey leftovers.

TURKEY and CRANBERRY PURSES

INGREDIENTS
serves six

450g | 1lb cooked turkey, cut into chunks

115g | 4oz | 1 cup diced Brie cheese

30ml | 2 tbsp cranberry sauce

30ml | 2 tbsp chopped fresh parsley

9 sheets of filo pastry, each measuring 45 x 28cm | 18 x 11in, thawed if frozen

50g | 2oz | 1¼ cups butter, melted

salt and ground black pepper

1 Preheat the oven to 200°C | 400°F | Gas 6. Place the turkey, Brie, cranberry sauce and chopped parsley in a small mixing bowl and mix well. Season with salt and pepper.

2 Cut the sheets of filo in half widthways and trim to make 18 squares. Keeping the remaining filo covered with clear film (plastic wrap) to prevent it from drying out, layer three pieces of pastry together, brushing each layer with a little melted butter. Repeat with the remaining filo squares to make 6 stacks.

3 Divide the turkey mixture evenly among the pastry stacks, making a neat pile in the centre of each piece. Gather up the pastry to enclose the filling in neat bundles. Place on a baking sheet, brush with melted butter and bake for about 20 minutes, or until the pastry is crisp and golden.

COOK'S TIP These little parcels can be made with a variety of fillings:
HAM AND CHEDDAR PURSES Replace the turkey with ham and use Cheddar cheese in place of the Brie. A fruit chutney would make a good alternative to the cranberry sauce.
CHICKEN AND STILTON PURSES Use cooked, diced chicken breast portions, white Stilton cheese and mango chutney.
GOAT'S CHEESE AND CELERY PURSES Use chopped celery and almonds, sautéed in a little butter, goat's cheese and chopped fresh figs.

Some of the most delicious dishes are also the simplest to make. Serve this popular pâté with warmed Melba toast as a first course, or for a light lunch with wholemeal toast.

SMOKED MACKEREL PÂTÉ

1 Break up the mackerel and put it in a food processor. Add the cream cheese, garlic, lemon juice and herbs.

2 Process the mixture until it is fairly smooth but still has a slightly chunky texture, then add Worcestershire sauce, salt and cayenne pepper to taste. Whizz to mix, then spoon the pâté into a dish, cover with clear film (plastic wrap) and chill. Garnish with chives and serve with Melba toast.

COOK'S TIP To make Melba toast, place some ready-sliced bread under a preheated grill (broiler) until browned on both sides. Cut off the crusts, and carefully slide the knife between the toasted edges to split the bread. Grill the uncooked sides again until the edges curl. The toast can be made in advance, and then reheated in a low oven.

VARIATION Use peppered mackerel fillets for a more piquant flavour. This pâté can also be made with smoked haddock or kipper fillets.

INGREDIENTS
serves six

4 smoked mackerel fillets, skinned

225g | 8oz | 1 cup cream cheese

1–2 garlic cloves, finely chopped

juice of 1 lemon

30ml | 2 tbsp chopped fresh chervil, parsley or chives

15ml | 1 tbsp Worcestershire sauce

salt and cayenne pepper

fresh chives, to garnish

warmed Melba toast, to serve

The combination of sweet beetroot, zesty orange and warm cinnamon in this salad is both unusual and delicious, and provides a lovely burst of colour in a winter buffet spread. It can be made with freshly steamed or pre-cooked beetroot.

BEETROOT SALAD with ORANGES

INGREDIENTS
serves four to six

675g | 1½lb beetroot (beet), steamed or boiled, then peeled

1 orange, peeled and sliced

30ml | 2 tbsp orange flower water

15ml | 1 tbsp sugar

5ml | 1 tsp ground cinnamon

salt and ground black pepper

1 Quarter the cooked beetroot, then slice the quarters. Arrange the beetroot on a plate with the orange slices or toss them together in a bowl.

2 Gently heat the orange flower water with the sugar, stir in the cinnamon and season to taste.

3 Pour the sweet mixture over the beetroot and orange salad and chill for at least 1 hour before serving.

COOK'S TIP To cook raw beetroot, always leave the skin on, and trim off only the tops of the leaf stalks. Cook in boiling water or steam over rapidly boiling water for 1–2 hours, depending on size. Small beetroots are tender in about 1 hour, medium roots take 1–1½ hours, and larger roots can take up to 2 hours.

Cook this vibrantly coloured dish in the oven at the same time as a pork casserole or a roast joint of meat for a simple, easy-to-prepare meal.

BRAISED RED CABBAGE with BEETROOT

INGREDIENTS
serves six to eight

675g | 1½lb red cabbage

1 Spanish onion, thinly sliced

30ml | 2 tbsp olive oil

2 tart eating apples, peeled, cored and sliced

300ml | ½ pint | 1¼ cups vegetable stock

60ml | 4 tbsp red wine vinegar

375g | 13oz raw beetroot (beet), peeled and coarsely grated

sea salt and ground black pepper

1 Cut the red cabbage into fine shreds, discarding any tough outer leaves and the core, and place in an ovenproof dish.

2 Place the thinly sliced onion and the olive oil in a frying pan and sauté until the onion is soft and golden.

3 Preheat the oven to 190°C | 375°F | Gas 5. Stir the apple slices, vegetable stock and wine vinegar into the onions, then transfer to the dish. Season with salt and pepper and cover.

4 Cook the cabbage for 1 hour. Stir in the beetroot, recover the dish and cook for a further 20–30 minutes, or until the cabbage and beetroot are tender.

COOK'S TIP When buying any type of cabbage, choose one that is firm and heavy for its size. The leaves should look healthy. Avoid any with curling leaves or blemishes.

This traditional Irish dish is the ultimate comfort food. Made with potatoes, onions and buttermilk, it is enriched with a wickedly indulgent amount of butter.

CHAMP

1 Boil the potatoes in lightly salted water for 20–25 minutes, until tender. Drain and mash with a fork until smooth.

2 Place the milk, spring onions and half the butter in a small pan and set over a low heat until just simmering. Cook for 2–3 minutes, until the butter has melted and the spring onions have softened.

3 Beat the milk mixture into the mashed potato using a wooden spoon. Beat in the buttermilk or crème fraîche until the mixture is light and fluffy. Reheat gently, adding salt and pepper to taste.

4 Turn the potato into a warmed serving dish and make a well in the centre with a spoon. Place the remaining butter in the well and let it melt. Serve immediately, sprinkled with extra spring onion.

VARIATIONS

COLCANNON This is another Irish speciality. Follow the main recipe, using half the butter. Cook about 500g | 1¼lb finely shredded green cabbage or kale in a little water until just tender, drain thoroughly and then beat into the creamed potato. This is delicious with sausages and grilled ham or bacon. It may also be fried in butter and then browned lightly under the grill (broiler).

CLAPSHOT To make this Scottish dish, halve the quantity of potato and replace with an equal weight (or slightly more) of swede (rutabaga). Use less butter and omit the buttermilk. Season with black pepper and plenty of freshly grated nutmeg. Traditionally, a chopped onion would be cooked with the potatoes and swede.

INGREDIENTS
serves four to six

1kg | 2¼lb boiling potatoes, cut into chunks

250ml | 8fl oz | 1 cup milk

1 bunch spring onions (scallions), thinly sliced, plus extra to garnish

115g | 4oz | ½ cup slightly salted butter

60ml | 4 tbsp buttermilk or crème fraîche

salt and ground black pepper

tasty and warm

Filling fare such as pulses and potatoes are combined with the zing of chilli, ginger and warming spices to make easy winter meals that will satisfy both the stomach and the tastebuds.

This is an easy dish, as black-eyed beans do not need to be soaked overnight. With spring onions and loads of aromatic dill, it is refreshing and healthy.

WARM SALAD with BLACK-EYED BEANS

INGREDIENTS
serves four

275g | 10oz | 1¹/₂ cups black-eyed beans (peas)

5 spring onions (scallions), sliced

a large handful of rocket (arugula) leaves, chopped if large

small cos (romaine) lettuce leaves

45–60ml | 3–4 tbsp chopped fresh dill

150ml | ¹/₄ pint | ²/₃ cup extra virgin olive oil

juice of 1 lemon, or more

10–12 black olives

salt and ground black pepper

1 Rinse and drain the beans, tip them into a pan and pour in cold water to cover. Bring to the boil, and strain immediately. Put them back in the pan with fresh cold water to cover, and add a pinch of salt. This will make their skins harder and prevent them from disintegrating when they are cooked.

2 Bring the beans to the boil, then lower the heat slightly and cook them until they are soft but not mushy. They will take 20–30 minutes, so keep an eye on them.

3 Drain the beans, reserving 75–90ml | 5–6 tbsp of the cooking liquid. Tip the beans into a large salad bowl, then add the remaining ingredients, including the reserved liquid, and mix well. Serve straight away as a warm salad, and serve with plenty of fresh, crusty bread.

VARIATION Rocket leaves have a peppery taste that complements the flavour of the beans, but watercress makes a good alternative, with an equally strong flavour.

Sweet parsnips, nutty chickpeas and zingy chilli and ginger paste combine to make a really tasty and filling dish, and will make a main meal when served with plain yogurt and warm naan bread or chapatis.

ZINGY PARSNIP and CHICKPEA CURRY

1 Put the soaked chickpeas in a pan, cover with cold water and bring to the boil. Boil vigorously for 10 minutes, then reduce the heat so that the water boils steadily. Cook for 1–1 1/2 hours, or until the chickpeas are tender. (The cooking time will depend on how long the chickpeas have been stored.) Drain and set aside.

2 Set 10ml | 2 tsp of the garlic aside, then place the remainder in a food processor or blender with the onion, ginger and half the chopped chillies. Add 75ml | 5 tbsp water and process to make a smooth paste.

3 Heat the oil in a frying pan and cook the cumin seeds for 30 seconds. Stir in the coriander seeds, turmeric, chilli powder or paprika and the ground cashew nuts. Mix in the ginger paste and cook, stirring frequently, until the water begins to evaporate. Add the tomatoes and stir-fry for 2–3 minutes.

4 Mix in the cooked chickpeas and parsnip chunks with 450ml | 3/4 pint | scant 2 cups water, a little salt and plenty of black pepper. Bring to the boil, stir, then simmer, uncovered, for 15–20 minutes, until the parsnips are completely tender.

5 Reduce the liquid, if necessary, by bringing the sauce to the boil and then boiling fiercely until the sauce is thick. Add the ground roasted cumin with more salt and lime juice to taste. Stir in the reserved garlic and green chilli, and cook for a further 1–2 minutes. Scatter the fresh coriander leaves and toasted cashew nuts over and serve straight away with yogurt and warmed naan bread or chapatis.

INGREDIENTS
serves four

200g | 7oz | 1 cup dried chickpeas, soaked overnight in cold water, then drained

7 garlic cloves, finely chopped

1 small onion, chopped

5cm | 2in piece fresh root ginger, chopped

2 green chillies, seeded and chopped

60ml | 4 tbsp sunflower oil

5ml | 1 tsp cumin seeds

10ml | 2 tsp ground coriander seeds

5ml | 1 tsp ground turmeric

2.5–5ml | 1/2–1 tsp chilli powder or mild paprika

50g | 2oz | 1/2 cup cashew nuts, toasted and ground

250g | 9oz tomatoes, peeled and chopped

900g | 2lb parsnips, cut into chunks

5ml | 1 tsp ground roasted cumin seeds

juice of 1 lime, to taste

chopped fresh coriander (cilantro) leaves and toasted whole cashew nuts, to garnish

These golden-brown, crisp potato cakes flavoured with onion, bacon and herbs are irresistible.

BACON and HERB RÖSTI

INGREDIENTS
serves four

450g | 1lb potatoes, left whole and unpeeled

30ml | 2 tbsp olive oil

1 red onion, finely chopped

4 back (lean) bacon rashers, rinded and diced

15ml | 1 tbsp potato flour

30ml | 2 tbsp chopped fresh mixed herbs

salt and ground black pepper

fresh parsley sprigs, to garnish

1 Lightly grease a baking sheet. Par-boil the potatoes in a pan of lightly salted, boiling water for about 6 minutes. Drain the potatoes and set aside to cool slightly.

2 Once cool enough to handle, peel the potatoes and coarsely grate them into a bowl. Set aside.

3 Heat 15ml | 1 tbsp of the oil in a frying pan, add the onion and bacon, and cook gently for 5 minutes, stirring occasionally. Preheat the oven to 220°C | 425°F | Gas 7.

4 Remove the pan from the heat. Stir the onion mixture, remaining oil, potato flour, herbs and seasoning into the grated potatoes and mix well.

5 Divide the mixture into 8 small piles and spoon them on to the prepared baking sheet, leaving a little space between each one.

6 Bake for 20–25 minutes until the rösti are crisp and golden brown. Serve immediately, garnished with sprigs of fresh parsley.

Subtly spiced with curry powder, turmeric, coriander and mild chilli powder, this rich gratin is substantial enough to serve on its own for lunch or supper. It also makes a good accompaniment to a larger meal.

VEGETABLE GRATIN with INDIAN SPICES

1 Thinly slice the potatoes, sweet potatoes and celeriac, using a sharp knife or the slicing attachment on a food processor. Immediately place the vegetables in a bowl of cold water to prevent them from discolouring.

2 Preheat the oven to 180°C | 350°F | Gas 4. Heat half the butter in a heavy pan, add the curry powder, turmeric and coriander and half of the chilli powder. Cook for 2 minutes, then leave to cool slightly. Drain the vegetables, then pat dry with kitchen paper. Place in a bowl, add the spice mixture and the shallots, and mix well.

3 Arrange the vegetables in a gratin dish, seasoning between the layers. Mix together the cream and milk, pour the mixture over the vegetables, then sprinkle the remaining chilli powder on top.

4 Cover with greaseproof (waxed) paper and bake for about 45 minutes. Remove the greaseproof paper, dot with the remaining butter and bake for a further 50 minutes, until the top is golden. Serve garnished with chopped fresh parsley.

COOK'S TIP The cream adds richness to this gratin. Use semi-skimmed (low-fat) milk if you prefer.

INGREDIENTS
serves four

2 large potatoes, total weight about 450g | 1lb

2 sweet potatoes, total weight about 275g | 10oz

175g | 6oz celeriac

15ml | 1 tbsp unsalted (sweet) butter

5ml | 1 tsp curry powder

5ml | 1 tsp ground turmeric

2.5ml | 1/2 tsp ground coriander

5ml | 1 tsp mild chilli powder

3 shallots, chopped

150ml | 1/4 pint | 2/3 cup single (light) cream

150ml | 1/4 pint | 2/3 cup milk

salt and ground black pepper

chopped fresh flat leaf parsley, to garnish

Serve this hearty butter-bean dish with grills, roasts, or fish. It is substantial enough to be served on its own, with a leafy salad and fresh, crusty bread. Bean dishes like this one often include a spicy sausage, such as Spanish chorizo. This can be added with the onion to lend its flavour to the whole dish.

TAGINE of BUTTER BEANS with OLIVES

INGREDIENTS
serves four

115g | 4oz | 2/3 cup butter (lima) beans, soaked overnight

30–45ml | 2–3 tbsp olive oil

1 onion, chopped

2–3 garlic cloves, crushed

25g | 1oz fresh root ginger, peeled and chopped

pinch of saffron threads

16 cherry tomatoes

generous pinch of sugar

handful of fleshy black olives, pitted

5ml | 1 tsp ground cinnamon

5ml | 1 tsp paprika

small bunch of flat leaf parsley

salt and ground black pepper

1 Rinse the beans and place them in a large pan with plenty of water. Bring to the boil and boil for about 10 minutes, then reduce the heat and simmer gently for 1–1½ hours, until tender. Drain the beans and refresh under cold water.

2 Heat the olive oil in a heavy pan. Add the onion, garlic and ginger and cook for about 10 minutes, or until softened but not browned. Stir in the saffron threads, followed by the cherry tomatoes and a sprinkling of sugar.

3 As the tomatoes begin to soften, stir in the butter beans. When the tomatoes have heated through, stir in the olives, ground cinnamon and paprika. Season to taste and sprinkle over the parsley. Serve immediately.

COOK'S TIP
If you are in a hurry, you could use two 400g | 14oz cans of butter beans for this tagine. Make sure you rinse the beans well, as canned beans tend to be salty.

hot and satisfying

Winter is the season for indulging the appetite for truly fulfilling dishes while entertaining friends and family. Rich gravies and tangy sauces accompany succulent roast meats and fish, pies and casseroles.

This classic dish originated in India. For a colourful garnish, add some finely sliced red onion or a little red onion marmalade.

KEDGEREE with SMOKED HADDOCK

INGREDIENTS
serves four

450g | 1lb undyed smoked haddock fillet

750ml | 1¹/₄ pints | 3 cups milk

2 bay leaves

¹/₂ lemon, sliced

50g | 2oz | ¹/₄ cup butter

1 onion, chopped

2.5ml | ¹/₂ tsp ground turmeric

5ml | 1 tsp mild Madras curry powder

2 green cardamom pods

350g | 12oz | 1³/₄ cups basmati or long grain rice, washed and drained

4 hard-boiled eggs (not too hard), roughly chopped

150ml | ¹/₄ pint | ²/₃ cup single (light) cream or Greek (US strained plain) yogurt (optional)

30ml | 2 tbsp chopped fresh parsley

salt and ground black pepper

1 Put the haddock in a shallow pan and add the milk, bay leaves and lemon slices. Poach gently for 8–10 minutes, until the haddock flakes easily when tested with the tip of a sharp knife. Strain the milk into a jug (pitcher), discarding the bay leaves and lemon slices. Remove the skin from the flesh of the haddock and flake the flesh into large pieces. Keep hot until required.

2 Melt the butter in the pan, add the onion and cook over a low heat for about 3 minutes, until softened. Stir in the turmeric, curry powder and cardamom pods and fry for 1 minute.

3 Add the rice, stirring to coat it well with the butter. Pour in the reserved milk, stir and bring to the boil. Lower the heat and simmer the rice for 10–12 minutes, until all the milk has been absorbed and the rice is tender. Season to taste, going easy on the salt.

4 Gently stir in the fish and hard-boiled eggs, with the cream or yogurt, if using. Sprinkle with the parsley and serve.

VARIATION Use smoked and poached fresh salmon for a delicious change.

This is a classic dish. It has layers of flavour, and the herbs add enticing aromas. Although it is made with economical ingredients (mussels are cheap compared to fish), it always produces spectacular results and is well worth the time it takes to prepare the seafood.

MUSSEL and RICE PILAFF

1 Discard any mussels that are not tightly shut, or which fail to snap shut when tapped. Place the remainder in a large heavy pan. Add about 1/3 of the onion slices, then pour in half of the wine and 150ml | 1/4 pint | 2/3 cup of the hot water. Cover and cook over a high heat for about 5 minutes, shaking the pan occasionally, until the mussels start to open.

2 Transfer the open mussels to a colander and collect their liquid in a bowl. Discard any mussels that remain closed. Shell most of the mussels, but keep a dozen or so large ones in their shells for decorative purposes. Let the liquid remaining in the pan settle, then carefully strain it through a lined sieve. Do the same with the liquid from the bowl, which drained from the cooked mussels.

3 Heat the olive oil in a heavy pan, add the remaining onion slices and the spring onions, and sauté over a medium heat until both start to turn golden. Add the garlic and oregano.

4 As soon as the garlic becomes aromatic, add the rice and stir briefly to coat the grains in the oil. Add the remaining wine, stirring until it has been absorbed, then stir in the remaining 300ml | 1/2 pint | 1 1/4 cups water, the reserved mussel liquid and the chopped parsley. Season with salt and pepper, then cover and cook gently for about 5 minutes, stirring occasionally.

5 Add the mussels, including the ones in their shells. Sprinkle in half of the dill and mix well. If necessary, add a little more hot water. Cover and cook gently for 5–6 minutes more, until the rice is cooked but still has a bit of bite at the centre of the grain. Sprinkle the remaining dill on top and serve with a green salad.

INGREDIENTS
serves four

1.6kg | 3 1/2lb mussels, scrubbed and bearded

2 onions, thinly sliced

2 glasses white wine, about 350ml | 12fl oz | 1 1/2 cups

450ml | 3/4 pint | scant 2 cups hot water

150ml | 1/4 pint | 2/3 cup extra virgin olive oil

5–6 spring onions (scallions), chopped

2 garlic cloves, chopped

large pinch of dried oregano

200g | 7oz | 1 cup long grain rice

45ml | 3 tbsp finely chopped fresh flat leaf parsley

45–60ml | 3–4 tbsp chopped fresh dill

salt and ground black pepper

The aroma of orange pervades many classic dishes, and the juice adds a distinctive flavour to wonderful fish recipes like this one. Red mullet is one of the fish that is still available from the Mediterranean in winter.

BAKED RED MULLET with ORANGES

INGREDIENTS
serves four

a few sprigs of fresh dill

4 large red mullet, total weight
1–1.2kg | 2¼–2½lb, cleaned

2 large oranges, halved

½ lemon

60ml | 4 tbsp extra virgin olive oil

30ml | 2 tbsp pine nuts

salt

1 Place some fresh dill in the cavity of each fish, and lay the fish in a baking dish, preferably one that can be taken straight to the table.

2 Set half an orange aside and squeeze the rest, along with the lemon. Mix the juice with the olive oil, then pour the mixture over the fish. Turn the fish so that they are evenly coated in the marinade, then cover and leave in a cool place to marinate for 1–2 hours, spooning the marinade over the fish occasionally.

3 Preheat the oven to 180°C | 350°F | Gas 4. Sprinkle a little salt over each fish. Slice the reserved orange half into thin rounds, then cut each round into quarters. Place two or three of these orange wedges over each fish. Bake for 20 minutes, then remove the dish from the oven, baste the fish with the juices and sprinkle the pine nuts over. Return the dish to the oven and bake for 10–15 minutes more.

VARIATION Bake oily sea fish such as herring and mackerel in a marinade made with lemons for a refreshing change.

A filling casserole of wonderfully tender chicken, root vegetables and lentils, finished with crème fraîche, mustard and tarragon, will warm you up on a cold winter's day.

CHICKEN CASSEROLE with WINTER VEGETABLES

INGREDIENTS
serves four

350g | 12oz onions

350g | 12oz leeks

225g | 8oz carrots

450g | 1lb swede (rutabaga)

30ml | 2 tbsp olive oil

4 chicken portions, about 900g | 2lb total weight

115g | 4oz | 1/2 cup green lentils

475ml | 16fl oz | 2 cups chicken stock

300ml | 1/2 pint | 1 1/4 cups apple juice

10ml | 2 tsp cornflour (cornstarch)

45ml | 3 tbsp crème fraîche

10ml | 2 tsp wholegrain mustard

30ml | 2 tbsp chopped fresh tarragon

salt and ground black pepper

fresh tarragon sprigs, to garnish

1 Preheat the oven to 190°C | 375°F | Gas 5. Prepare and chop the vegetables.

2 Heat the oil in a large flameproof casserole. Season the chicken portions and brown them in the hot oil until golden. Remove the chicken from the pan.

3 Add the onions to the casserole and cook for 5 minutes, stirring, until they begin to soften and colour. Add the leeks, carrots, swede and lentils to the casserole and stir over a medium heat for 2 minutes.

4 Return the chicken to the pan, then add the stock, apple juice and seasoning. Bring to the boil and cover tightly. Cook in the oven for 50–60 minutes, or until the chicken and lentils are tender.

5 Place the casserole on the hob (stovetop) over a medium heat. In a small bowl, blend the cornflour with about 30ml | 2 tbsp water to make a smooth paste, and add to the casserole with the crème fraîche, wholegrain mustard and chopped tarragon. Adjust the seasoning, then simmer gently for about 2 minutes, stirring, until thickened slightly. Serve, garnished with tarragon sprigs.

COOK'S TIP Chop the vegetables into similarly sized pieces so that they cook evenly. Organic vegetables do not need peeling.

A succulent roast goose is the classic centrepiece for a traditional winter family dinner. Juicy red cabbage cooked with leeks, and braised fennel are tasty and colourful accompaniments.

MARMALADE-GLAZED GOOSE with STUFFING

1 Preheat the oven to 200°C | 400°F | Gas 6. Prick the skin of the goose all over and season it inside and out. Mix the apple, onion and sage leaves together and spoon the mixture into the parson's nose end of the goose.

2 To make the stuffing, melt the butter or oil in a large pan and cook the onion for about 5 minutes, or until softened but not coloured. Remove the pan from the heat and stir in the marmalade, chopped prunes, Madeira, breadcrumbs and chopped sage.

3 Stuff the neck end of the goose with the stuffing. Sew up the bird or secure it with skewers to prevent the stuffing from escaping during cooking.

4 Place the goose in a large roasting pan. Butter a piece of foil and use to cover the goose loosely, then roast in the preheated oven for 2 hours.

5 Baste the goose frequently during cooking and remove any excess fat from the pan as necessary, using a small ladle or serving spoon. (Strain, cool and chill the fat in a covered container: it is excellent for roasting potatoes.)

6 Remove the foil from the goose and brush the melted ginger marmalade over the goose, then roast for 30–40 minutes more, or until cooked through. To check if the goose is cooked, pierce the thick part of the thigh with a metal skewer; the juices will run clear when the bird is cooked. Remove from the oven and cover with foil, then leave to stand for 15 minutes before carving.

INGREDIENTS
serves eight

4.5kg | 10lb goose

1 cooking apple, peeled, cored and cut into eighths

1 large onion, cut into eighths

bunch of fresh sage, plus extra to garnish

30ml/2 tbsp ginger marmalade, melted

salt and ground black pepper

for the stuffing

25g | 1oz | 2 tbsp butter or 30ml | 2 tbsp olive oil

1 onion, finely chopped

15ml | 1 tbsp ginger marmalade

450g | 1lb | 2 cups ready-to-eat prunes, chopped

45ml | 3 tbsp Madeira

225g | 8oz | 4 cups fresh white or wholemeal (whole-wheat) breadcrumbs

30ml | 2 tbsp chopped fresh sage

William the Conqueror introduced cider-making to England from Normandy in 1066. This wonderful old West Country ham glazed with cider is traditionally served with cranberry sauce.

SOMERSET CIDER-GLAZED HAM

1 Weigh the ham and calculate the cooking time at 20 minutes per 450g │ 1lb, and then place it in a large pan. Stud the onion or onions with half of the cloves and add to the pan with the bay leaves and peppercorns.

2 Add 1.2 litres │ 2 pints │ 5 cups of the cider and enough water to cover the ham. Heat until simmering and then carefully skim off the scum that rises to the surface, using a large spoon or ladle. Time the cooking from the moment the stock begins to simmer. Cover with a lid or foil and simmer gently for the calculated time. Towards the end of the cooking time, preheat the oven to 220°C │ 425° │ Gas 7.

3 Heat the sugar and remaining cider in a pan; stir until the sugar has dissolved. Simmer for 5 minutes to make a dark, sticky glaze. Remove the pan from the heat and leave to cool for 5 minutes. Lift the ham out of the pan, using a draining spoon and a large fork. Carefully and evenly, cut the rind from the ham, then score the fat into a neat diamond pattern. Place the ham in a roasting pan or ovenproof dish. Press a clove into the centre of each diamond, then carefully spoon over the glaze. Bake for 20–25 minutes, or until the fat is brown, glistening and crisp.

4 Simmer all the cranberry sauce ingredients in a heavy-based pan for 15–20 minutes, stirring frequently. Transfer the sauce to a jug. Serve the ham hot or cold, garnished with parsley and with the cranberry sauce.

VARIATION Use honey in place of the soft brown sugar for the glaze, and serve the ham with redcurrant sauce or jelly.

INGREDIENTS
serves eight to ten

2kg │ 4¹/₂lb middle gammon joint

1 large or 2 small onions

about 30 whole cloves

3 bay leaves

10 black peppercorns

1.3 litres │ 2¹/₄ pints │ 5²/₃ cups medium-dry cider

45ml │ 3 tbsp soft light brown sugar

bunch of flat leaf parsley, to garnish

for the cranberry sauce

350g │ 12oz │ 3 cups cranberries

175g │ 6oz │ ³/₄ cup soft light brown sugar

grated rind and juice of 2 clementines

30ml │ 2 tbsp port

This hearty winter dish has a rich Guinness gravy and a herb pastry top. The Stilton adds a delicious creaminess but can be left out to make a less rich version of the pie.

CHESTNUT, STILTON and GUINNESS PIE

INGREDIENTS
serves four

2 large onions, chopped

500g | 1¼lb | 8 cups button mushrooms

3 carrots and 1 parsnip, sliced

15ml | 1 tbsp fresh thyme

2 bay leaves

250ml | 8fl oz | 1 cup Guinness

120ml | 4fl oz | ½ cup vegetable stock

5ml | 1tbsp Worcestershire sauce

5ml | 1 tsp soft dark brown sugar

350g | 12oz | 3 cups canned chestnuts

30ml | 2 tbsp plain (all-purpose) flour

150g | 5oz | 1¼ cups Stilton cheese

salt and freshly ground black pepper

for the pastry

115g | 4oz | 1 cup wholemeal (whole-wheat) flour

50g | 2oz | 4 tbsp unsalted butter

15ml | 1 tbsp fresh thyme

1 egg, beaten, or milk, to glaze

1 To make the pastry, rub together the flour, salt and butter or margarine until the mixture resembles fine breadcrumbs. Add the thyme and enough water to form a soft dough. Turn out the dough on to a floured board or work surface and gently knead for 1 minute until it forms a smooth dough. Wrap in clear film (plastic wrap) and chill for 30 minutes.

2 Meanwhile, to make the filling, heat 2 tbsp of sunflower oil in a heavy pan and fry the onions for 5 minutes until softened, stirring occasionally. Halve the mushrooms, add and cook for a further 3 minutes or until just tender. Add the carrots, parsnip and herbs, stir and cover the pan. Cook for three minutes until slightly softened.

3 Pour in the Guinness, vegetable stock and Worcestershire sauce, then add the sugar and seasoning. Simmer, covered, for 5 minutes, stirring occasionally. Halve the chestnuts and add.

4 Mix the flour to a paste with 30ml | 2 tbsp water. Add to the Guinness mixture and cook, uncovered, for 5 minutes, until the sauce thickens, stirring. Stir in the cheese and heat until melted, stirring constantly.

5 Preheat the oven to 220°C | 425° | Gas 7. Roll out the pastry to fit the top of a 1.5 litre | 2½ pint | 6¼ cup deep pie dish. Spoon the chestnut mixture into the dish. Dampen the edges of the dish and cover with the pastry. Seal, trim and crimp the edges. Cut a small slit in the top of the pie and use any surplus pastry to make pastry leaves. Brush with egg or milk and bake for 30 minutes until the pastry is golden.

Low in fat but high in flavour, venison is an excellent choice for a healthy, yet rich, casserole. Cranberries and orange bring fruitiness to this spicy recipe.

SPICY VENISON CASSEROLE

1 Heat the oil in a flameproof casserole. Add the onion and celery and sauté for about 5 minutes, until softened.

2 Meanwhile, mix the ground allspice with the flour and either spread the mixture out on a large plate or place in a large plastic bag. Toss a few pieces of venison at a time (to prevent them from becoming soggy) in the flour mixture until they are all lightly coated.

3 When the onion and celery are softened, remove from the casserole using a slotted spoon and set aside. Add the venison pieces to the casserole in batches and cook until browned and sealed on all sides.

4 Add the cranberries, orange rind and juice to the casserole along with the beef or venison stock and stir well. Return the vegetables and all the venison to the casserole and heat until simmering, then cover tightly and reduce the heat. Simmer for about 45 minutes, until the venison is tender, stirring occasionally.

5 Season to taste with salt and pepper before serving.

VARIATION Farmed venison is increasingly easy to find and is available at good butchers and many large supermarkets. It makes a rich and flavourful stew, but lean pork or braising steak could be used instead of the venison if you prefer. You could also replace the cranberries with pitted and halved prunes, and, for extra flavour, use either ale or stout instead of about half the stock.

INGREDIENTS
serves four

30ml | 2 tbsp olive oil

1 onion, chopped

2 celery stalks, sliced

10ml | 2 tsp ground allspice

15ml | 1 tbsp plain (all-purpose) flour

675g | 1½lb stewing venison, cubed

225g | 8oz fresh or frozen cranberries

grated rind and juice of 1 orange

900ml | 1½ pints | 3¾ cups beef or venison stock

salt and ground black pepper

Cassoulet is a very hearty, one-pot meal of white beans, preserved meats and sausage. The method of adding each meat at different stages to the simmering pot of beans and flavourings is crucial to the finished dish. This is a great dish to make in advance – traditionally it can go on bubbling for days.

BUTTER BEAN CASSOULET with DUCK

INGREDIENTS
serves six to eight

675g | 1½lb | 3¾ cups dried butter (lima) beans

2 large onions, sliced

6 large garlic cloves, crushed

3 bay leaves

10ml | 2 tsp dried thyme

2 whole cloves

60ml | 4 tbsp tomato purée (paste)

12 sun-dried tomatoes in oil, drained and roughly chopped

450g | 1lb smoked pancetta

60ml | 4 tbsp olive oil

4 boneless duck breasts

12 Toulouse or chunky Italian sausages

400g | 14oz can plum tomatoes

75g | 3oz | 1½ cups stale white breadcrumbs

salt and ground black pepper

1 Put the beans in a large bowl, cover with plenty of cold water and leave to soak for several hours or overnight.

2 Drain the beans well and tip into a large pan. Cover with fresh water and bring to the boil. Boil rapidly for 10 minutes to destroy any indigestible enzymes, then drain well and tip into a large flameproof casserole. Add the onions, garlic, bay leaves, dried thyme, cloves, tomato purée and sun-dried tomatoes.

3 Trim the rind from the pancetta and cut into large pieces. Heat about 30ml | 2 tbsp of the oil in a frying pan and brown the pancetta in batches. Stir it into the casserole and add enough water to cover. Bring to the boil, then reduce the heat so that it just simmers. Cover and simmer for about 1½ hours, until the beans are tender.

4 Preheat the oven to 180°C | 350°F | Gas 4. Score the skin of the duck breasts, then cut each breast into large pieces. Cut each sausage into three pieces. Heat the remaining oil in a frying pan and fry the duck, skin side down, until golden-brown, then transfer to the casserole. Lightly fry the sausages in the remaining fat and stir into the beans with the canned tomatoes, adding salt and pepper to taste.

5 Sprinkle the breadcrumbs in an even layer over the surface of the cassoulet and bake for 45–60 minutes, or until a golden crust has formed. Serve warm.

Long, slow cooking is the trick to remember for good onion gravy, as this reduces and caramelizes the onions to create a wonderfully sweet flavour. Do not be alarmed by the number of onions – they reduce dramatically in volume during cooking.

SAUSAGES with MASH and ONION GRAVY

1 Heat the oil and butter in a large pan until foaming. Add the onions and mix well to coat them in the fat. Cover and cook gently for about 30 minutes, stirring frequently. Add the sugar and cook for another 5 minutes, or until the onions are softened, reduced and caramelized.

2 Remove the pan from the heat and stir in the flour, then gradually stir in the stock. Return the pan to the heat. Bring to the boil, stirring, then simmer for 3 minutes, or until thickened. Season.

3 Meanwhile, cook the potatoes and the pork and leek sausages. First, cook the potatoes in a pan of boiling salted water for 20 minutes, or until tender.

4 Drain the potatoes well and mash them with the butter, cream and wholegrain mustard. Season with salt and pepper to taste.

5 While the potatoes are cooking, preheat the grill (broiler) to medium. Arrange the sausages in a single layer in the broiler pan and cook for 15–20 minutes or until cooked through, turning frequently so that they brown evenly.

6 Serve the sausages with the mashed potatoes and plenty of onion gravy.

INGREDIENTS
serves four

12 pork and leek sausages

salt and ground black pepper

for the onion gravy

30ml | 2 tbsp olive oil

30ml | 2 tbsp butter

8 onions, sliced

5ml | 1 tsp sugar

15ml | 1 tbsp plain (all-purpose) flour

300ml | 1/2 pint | 11/4 cups beef stock

for the mashed potatoes

1.4kg | 31/4lb potatoes, peeled and cut into chunks

50g | 2oz | 1/4 cup butter

150ml | 1/4 pint | 2/3 cup double (heavy) cream

15ml/1 tbsp wholegrain mustard

rich and filling

On a cold day, there's nothing like the indulgence of a steaming, golden sponge pudding, flavoured with maple syrup, or hot poached fruits spiced with cloves and cinnamon. The seasonal combination of chocolate and orange makes winter worth waiting for.

Imagine a hot sponge cake, straight out of the oven but with less golden crust, a deeper sponge and more crumbliness – that's a steamed pudding. It can be flavoured with anything – maple syrup and pecan nuts are wonderful, and look superb when turned out, as here. Serve with lots of your own home-made custard.

STICKY MAPLE and PECAN PUDDING

INGREDIENTS
serves six

60ml | 4 tbsp pure maple syrup

30ml | 2 tbsp fresh brown breadcrumbs

115g | 4oz | 1 cup shelled pecan nuts, roughly chopped

115g | 4oz | 1/2 cup butter, softened

finely grated rind of 1 orange

115g | 4oz | heaped 1/2 cup golden caster (superfine) sugar

2 eggs, beaten

175g | 6oz | 1 1/2 cups self-raising (self-rising) flour, sifted

pinch of salt

about 75ml | 5 tbsp milk

extra maple syrup and home-made custard, to serve

1 Butter a 900ml | 1 1/2 pint | 3 3/4 cup heatproof pudding bowl generously. Stir the maple syrup, breadcrumbs and pecans together and spoon into the bowl.

2 Cream the butter with the orange rind and sugar until light and fluffy. Gradually beat in the eggs, then fold in the flour and salt. Stir in enough milk to make a loose mixture that will drop off the spoon if lightly shaken.

3 Carefully spoon the mixture into the bowl on top of the syrup and nuts. Cover with pleated, buttered baking parchment, then with pleated foil (the pleats allow for expansion). Tie string under the lip of the basin to hold the paper in place, then take it over the top to form a handle.

4 Place the bowl in a pan of simmering water, cover and steam for 2 hours, topping up with boiling water as necessary. Remove the string, foil and paper, then turn out the pudding and serve with extra maple syrup and custard.

COOK'S TIP To make your own pouring custard:
1 Heat 450ml | 3/4 pint | scant 2 cups milk with a few drops of vanilla essence and remove from the heat just as the it comes to the boil. Whisk 2 eggs and 1 yolk in a bowl with 30ml | 2 tbsp caster (superfine) sugar. Blend together 15ml | 1 tbsp cornflour (cornstarch) with 30ml | 2 tbsp water and mix with the eggs. Whisk in a little of the hot milk, then add the rest.

2 Strain the egg and milk mixture back into the pan and heat gently, stirring frequently, until the custard thickens sufficiently to coat the back of a wooden spoon.

Fresh apples and pears are combined with dried apricots and figs, and cooked in a fragrant, spicy wine until tender and intensely flavoured.

WINTER FRUIT POACHED in MULLED WINE

INGREDIENTS
serves four

300ml | 1/2 pint | 1 1/4 cups red wine

300ml | 1/2 pint | 1 1/4 cups fresh orange juice

finely grated rind and juice of 1 orange

45ml | 3 tbsp clear honey or barley malt syrup

1 cinnamon stick, broken in half

4 cloves

4 cardamom pods, split

2 pears, such as Comice or William, peeled, cored and halved

8 ready-to-eat dried figs

12 ready-to-eat dried unsulphured apricots

2 eating apples, peeled, cored and thickly sliced

1 Put the wine, the fresh and squeezed orange juice and half the orange rind in a pan with the honey or syrup and spices. Bring to the boil, then reduce the heat and simmer for 2 minutes, stirring occasionally.

2 Add the pears, figs and apricots to the pan and cook, covered, for 25 minutes, occasionally turning the fruit in the wine mixture. Add the sliced apples and cook for a further 12–15 minutes, until the fruit is tender.

3 Remove the fruit from the pan and discard the spices. Cook the wine mixture over a high heat until reduced and syrupy, then pour it over the fruit. Serve decorated with the reserved strips of orange rind, if wished.

COOK'S TIP Serve with fresh cream, custard, or rice pudding.

This creamy pudding is scented with saffron, cardamom and freshly grated nutmeg. Shelled pistachio nuts give a subtle contrast in colour and add crunch.

INDIAN RICE PUDDING

1 Wash the rice under cold running water and place in a pan with the boiling water. Bring to the boil and boil, uncovered, for 15 minutes.

2 Pour the milk over the rice, then reduce the heat and simmer, partially covered, for 15 minutes.

3 Add the cardamom pods, grated nutmeg, saffron, maize malt syrup and honey, and cook for a further 15 minutes, or until the rice is tender, stirring occasionally.

4 Spoon the rice into small serving bowls and sprinkle with pistachio nuts before serving hot or cold.

COOK'S TIP Rice pudding is delicious served with fresh or dried fruit. Try it with the Winter Fruit Poached in Mulled Wine.

INGREDIENTS
serves four

115g | 4oz | 3/4 cup brown short grain rice

350ml | 12fl oz | 1 1/2 cups boiling water

600ml | 1 pint | 2 1/2 cups milk

6 cardamom pods, bruised

2.5ml | 1/2 tsp freshly grated nutmeg

pinch of saffron threads

60ml | 4 tbsp maize malt syrup

15ml | 1 tbsp clear honey

50g | 2oz | 1/2 cup pistachio nuts, chopped

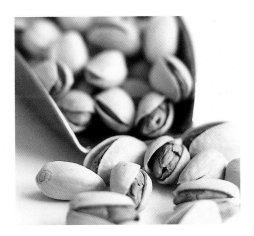

Everything about this mousse is seductive. The smooth, creamy chocolate lingers on the tongue long after being eaten. Only the best chocolates have this effect, so save your most expensive, cocoa-solids-packed variety for this ultimate indulgence.

CHOCOLATE, ORANGE and LIQUEUR MOUSSE

1 Break the chocolate into pieces and put in a small bowl over a pan of barely simmering water. Pour in the liqueur and add the butter. Leave undisturbed for about 10 minutes, until melted.

2 Separate the eggs and put the whites into a large mixing bowl with a tiny pinch of salt. Stir the chocolate mixture and remove from the heat. Quickly mix in the egg yolks.

3 Whisk the egg whites until stiff but not dry. Fold one large spoonful into the chocolate sauce to loosen the mixture, then carefully, but thoroughly, fold in the remaining egg whites.

4 Spoon the mixture into little pots or ramekins, cover and chill for at least 6 hours, or until set. Serve with thin strips of crystallized orange peel.

INGREDIENTS
serves four

200g | 7oz orange-flavoured dark (bittersweet) chocolate with more than 60% cocoa solids

45ml | 3 tbsp Grand Marnier liqueur

25g/ | 1oz | 2 tbsp unsalted (sweet) butter

3 large (US extra large) eggs

salt

crystallized (candied) orange peel, to serve

This combination of intense flavours produces a very rich dessert, so serve it well chilled and in thin slices. It slices better when it is very cold.

CHOCOLATE CHESTNUT ROULADE

INGREDIENTS
serves ten to twelve

oil, for greasing

175g | 6oz dark chocolate, chopped

30ml | 2 tbsp unsweetened cocoa powder, sifted, plus extra for dusting

50ml | 2fl oz | 1/4 cup freshly brewed strong coffee or espresso

6 eggs, separated

75g | 3oz | 6 tbsp caster (superfine) sugar

pinch of cream of tartar

5ml | 1 tsp vanilla essence (extract)

glacé (candied) chestnuts, to decorate

thick cream, to serve

for the chestnut cream filling

475ml | 16fl oz | 2 cups double (heavy) cream

30ml | 2 tbsp rum or coffee-flavoured liqueur

350g | 12oz can sweetened chestnut purée

115g | 4oz dark chocolate, grated

1 Preheat the oven to 180°C | 350°F | Gas 4. Grease the base and sides of a 39x27x2.5cm | 15 1/2x10 1/2x1in Swiss roll tin (jelly roll pan). Line with baking parchment, allowing a 2.5cm | 1in overhang.

2 Melt the chocolate in the top of a double boiler over a low heat, stirring frequently. Mix the cocoa with the coffee and set aside. In an electric mixer or in a bowl using a whisk, beat the egg yolks with half of the sugar for about 3–5 minutes, until pale and thick. Slowly beat in the melted chocolate and cocoa-coffee paste until just blended.

3 In another bowl, whisk the egg whites and cream of tartar until stiff peaks form. Sprinkle the remaining sugar over in two batches and beat until stiff and glossy, then beat in the vanilla essence. Stir a spoonful of the whisked whites into the chocolate mixture to lighten it, then fold in the remainder. Spoon the mixture into the tin and level the top. Bake for 20–25 minutes, or until the cake springs back when lightly pressed.

4 Meanwhile, dust a clean dishtowel with the extra cocoa powder. As soon as the cake is cooked, carefully turn it out on to the towel and gently peel off the baking parchment from the base. Starting at a narrow end, roll the cake and towel together and cool.

5 To make the filling, whip the cream and rum or liqueur until soft peaks form. Beat a spoonful of cream into the chestnut purée, then fold in the remaining cream and most of the grated chocolate. Unroll the cake and spread 3/4 of the filling to within 2.5cm | 1in of the edges. Gently roll it up, using the towel for support and place seam-side down, on a serving plate. Spoon the reserved chestnut cream into a small icing bag and pipe rosettes along the top. Decorate with glacé chestnuts, grated chocolate and cocoa.

When kumquats are in season, their marvellous spicy-sweet citrus flavour complements both sweet and savoury dishes.

SPICED POACHED KUMQUATS

INGREDIENTS
serves six

450g | 1lb | 4 cups kumquats

115g | 4oz | generous 1/2 cup unrefined caster (superfine) sugar or rapadura

150ml | 1/4 pint | 2/3 cup water

1 small cinnamon stick

1 star anise

1 bay leaf, to decorate (optional)

1 Cut the kumquats in half and discard the pips. Place the kumquats in a pan with the sugar, water and spices. Cook over a gentle heat, stirring until the sugar has dissolved.

2 Increase the heat, cover the pan and boil the mixture for 8-10 minutes, until the kumquats are tender. To bottle the kumquats, spoon them into warm, sterilized jars, seal and label. Decorate the kumquats with a bay leaf before serving, if you like.

COOK'S TIP To prepare jars for home preserves, preheat the oven to 160°C | 325°F | Gas 3. Wash the jars in hot soapy water, rinse and dry thoroughly. Place the jars in the oven for 10 minutes, then turn off the oven and leave to cool.

The combination of light Italian fruit bread, apricots and pecan nuts produces a wonderfully rich version of traditional bread-and-butter pudding.

APRICOT PANETTONE PUDDING

1 Grease a 1 litre | 1³/₄ pint | 4 cup baking dish. Arrange half the panettone in the base of the dish, scatter over half the pecan nuts and all the dried apricots, then add another layer of panettone on top, spreading it as evenly as you can.

2 Pour the milk into a small pan and add the vanilla essence. Warm the milk over a medium heat until it just simmers. In a large bowl, mix together the beaten egg and maple syrup, grate in the nutmeg, then whisk in the hot milk.

3 Preheat the oven to 200°C | 400°F | Gas 6. Pour the milk mixture over the panettone, lightly pressing down each slice so that it is totally submerged in the mixture. Set the dish aside and leave the pudding to stand for at least 10 minutes.

4 Scatter the reserved pecan nuts over the top and sprinkle with the demerara sugar and nutmeg. Bake for about 40 minutes, until risen and golden.

COOK'S TIP Panettone is a sweet Italian yeast bread made with raisins, citron, pine nuts and star anise. If it is not available, use any sweet yeasted fruit loaf instead.

INGREDIENTS
serves six

unsalted (sweet) butter, for greasing

350g | 12oz panettone, sliced into triangles

25g | 1oz | ¹/₄ cup pecan nuts

75g | 3oz | ¹/₃ cup ready-to-eat dried apricots, chopped

500ml | 17fl oz | 2¹/₄ cups semi-skimmed (low-fat) milk

5ml | 1 tsp vanilla essence

1 large egg, beaten

30ml | 2 tbsp maple syrup

2.5ml | ¹/₂ tsp grated nutmeg, plus extra for sprinkling

demerara (raw) sugar, for sprinkling

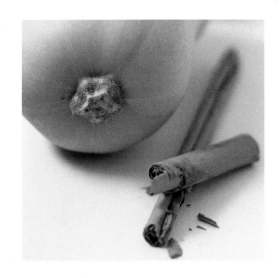

The bright orange colour and warming flavour of this marmalade is guaranteed to banish the winter blues.

PUMPKIN and ORANGE MARMALADE

1 Squeeze the juice from the oranges, remove the membranes and reserve with the pips (seeds). Thinly slice the peel and place in a large pan with the sliced lemons. Tie the pips and membranes in a muslin (cheesecloth) bag with the spices. Add to the citrus fruit with the water. Bring to the boil, then cover and simmer for 1 hour, or until the fruit is tender.

2 Add the pumpkin and continue cooking for 1½ hours, or until very tender. Remove the muslin bag, squeeze out over the pan and then discard.

3 Stir in the sugar over a low heat until completely dissolved. Increase the heat and boil for a further 10–15 minutes, or until the marmalade becomes quite thick and reaches setting point.

4 Remove the pan from the heat and skim off any scum from the surface using a slotted spoon. Leave to cool for 5 minutes then pour into warm sterilized jars. Seal and label, then store in a cool, dark place.

COOK'S TIP To test for the setting point, spoon a small quantity on to a chilled saucer, chill for 3 minutes, then push the mixture with your finger. If wrinkles form on the surface, it is ready. Alternatively, you could use a sugar thermometer clipped to the side of the pan, but not touching the base. When the temperature reaches 105°C|220°F, the marmalade is ready.

INGREDIENTS
makes 2.75kg | 6lb

900g | 2lb Seville (Temple) oranges, washed and halved

450g | 1lb lemons, halved and thinly sliced

2 cinnamon sticks

2.5cm | 1in piece fresh root ginger, peeled and thinly sliced

1.5ml | ¼ tsp grated nutmeg

1.75 litres | 3 pints | 7½ cups water

800g | 1¾lb pumpkin, peeled, seeds (pips) removed and thinly sliced

1.3kg | 3lb | 6¾ cups warmed sugar

INDEX